How Do Governments Spend Money?

T0016084

Antonio Sacre, M.A.

Reader Consultants

Brian Allman, M.A.
Classroom Teacher, West Virginia

Cynthia Donovan
Classroom Teacher, California

iCivics Consultants

Emma Humphries, Ph.D.
Chief Education Officer

Taylor Davis, M.T.
Director of Curriculum and Content

Natacha Scott, MAT
Director of Educator Engagement

Publishing Credits

Rachelle Cracchiolo, M.S.Ed., *Publisher*
Emily R. Smith, M.A.Ed., *VP of Content Development*
Véronique Bos, *Creative Director*
Dona Herweck Rice, *Senior Content Manager*
Dani Neiley, *Associate Editor*
Fabiola Sepulveda, *Series Designer*
Marina Pessarrodona, *Illustrator, pages 6–9*

Image Credits: p10 Alamy/Tami Chappell; p10 middle Official South Carolina Governor's Office Photo by Sam Holland; p10 right Shutterstock/Mark Reinstein; p13 Alamy/Zev Radovan/BibleLandPictures; p15 Associated Press; p18 Alamy/MC2 Ridge Leoni; p22 Shutterstock/Erika J Mitchell; p23 Alamy/David Grossman; p24 Shutterstock/Matt Bannister; p26 Alamy/agefotostock; all other images from iStock and/or Shutterstock

5482 Argosy Avenue
Huntington Beach, CA 92649
www.tcmpub.com

ISBN 978-1-0876-1544-8

Table of Contents

Grandma's Gift

For your birthday, your grandmother mails you a birthday card. When you open it, a crisp, clean $20 bill falls to the table. Inside, she writes a sweet note that ends with, "Here's a little something just for you!"

Now you have a decision to make. What do you do with the money? You could spend, save, or invest it. You could even give it away. It's your money, and you can do whatever you want with it.

If you want to buy something that costs more than $20, you'll have to think about how to get the rest of the money. Maybe you have some in your piggy bank. Maybe you can earn some money selling lemonade.

When the **government** gets money, it has similar decisions to make. But how does the government get money in the first place? What is that money spent on? And if the government needs more, where does it come from?

Jump into Fiction

The Dunk Tank

Anthony and his best friend, Camila, survey the set-up for their school fundraiser. The whole playground had been changed into a huge pumpkin patch with hay bales and pumpkins everywhere. Parents and volunteers stand at face-painting booths, craft areas, food tables, the haunted maze, and the most important spot: the dunk tank.

Anthony points at a poster and says, "Camila, check it out. The first teacher gets in the tank at one o'clock. And guess what? It's Ms. Vargas!"

"Well, I'm using my money to try to dunk the principal. What time does he go in?" she asks.

"He goes in at two o'clock. I'll have to make sure I save some money!"

Camila looks more closely at the sign. "It's $1 a throw or $5 for six chances."

"My grandma gave me $20 for my birthday. I want to make sure I have enough to buy some food and to dunk our teacher!" exclaims Anthony.

A line of students forms by the dunk tank, eagerly waiting their turn. Anthony yells, "Look at Ms. Vargas! She's wearing goggles and a yellow floatie!"

Ms. Vargas climbs the ladder and perches on the platform above the tank. "Remember, this event is fun, but more importantly, it's about raising money. The state cut our budget, and we need to purchase books and new sports equipment. Plus, I want to stay *dry*," she laughs.

A first grader gives his money to the parent volunteer in front, and he lobs a ball way off target.

Camila leans to Anthony and asks, "Why did the state take our money?"

"I don't know. My mom said they took it from all schools around the state. It's about a budget something or other," Anthony responds.

"Oh yeah. I remember my parents talking, and they called it a budget deficit. I guess it means there's not enough money."

"Well, at least this will help raise money. Are you ready, Ms. V?" Anthony adds with a laugh as he steps up for his turn.

Ms. Vargas looks up with a grin. "Give it your best shot!" she calls back, just as Anthony's throw connects and she hits the water with a splash!

Back to Nonfiction

Levels of Government and Money

There are three main levels of government in the United States. They are local, state, and federal. Each type needs money to function.

A government serves a community. The bigger the community, the bigger the government. A school board supports one school district. A city council supports one city. A governor supports one state. A president supports one country.

Smaller groups form local governments. These can be towns, cities, or counties. Leaders of these groups may be mayors.

local

Kasim Reed
Atlanta mayor

state

Nikki Haley
South Carolina governor

federal

George H. W. Bush
president of the
United States

Who Makes Money?

The U.S. Department of Treasury prints paper money and mints coins. Each year, about seven billion banknotes are printed. This replaces money that is worn out or lost. And every year, about $62 million in coins is lost!

Local governments in the Unites States must follow the rules of their state governments. Leaders of state governments are governors.

All the states combined form a nation. Leaders of nations may be prime ministers or chancellors. In the United States, it is the president.

Governments make laws and solve problems. To operate, they need money. They raise money through taxes. Once they raise money, they spend it. In a **democracy**, people have a say in how the money is spent, although they usually do not make the final decisions. Sometimes, a community has a number of issues that need money. The government may have to choose which issues to support. There might not be enough money for all. So, what do they do?

Local Governments

Local governments often run fire departments, hospitals, and schools. If firefighters need a new firehouse, they ask the local government. The same goes for public hospitals or schools. If they need new wings or buildings, they ask the local government.

As long as the local government has the money to help, issues like these can be solved. But what if the government has money to help with only some needs? What if it has *no* money for any of these needs?

The government might wait to help until it raises enough money. It might even stop helping. In some places, things such as libraries and parks get closed down when there isn't enough money. Street repairs stop. Workers get laid off, or let go from their jobs.

Local citizens don't like when these things happen. Elected leaders can lose their jobs when the people are unhappy by not being reelected. So, the government tries to find ways to solve the issues. It might ask the people if they would pay more taxes. This could raise more money. If the people say no, the local government can ask the state for money to help. If the state is able to help, the problem is solved!

The Lydian Lion

Before there was money, people traded things as payment. Coins made trade easier. The first coin ever minted had a roaring lion on it. It is called the Lydian Lion. It was made more than 2,500 years ago.

State Governments

Just like local ones, state governments need to raise money for expenses. Expenses can be anything from building new highways to caring for the environment. But where does the money come from? A lot of it comes from taxes. There are many types of taxes, including **property tax**, **sales tax**, and **income tax**. Money also comes from fees and licenses.

RECEIPT
THANK YOU

02/21   3:31PM   04
000000#1798

SANDWICH $7.50
TAX $0.66

ITEMS   1
CHARGE $8.16

PLEASE
VISIT
US AGAIN

Government Salaries

The president is paid over $400,000 a year to be president. Most governors make at least $100,000 each year. Federal judges make more than $200,000 a year. Members of Congress make at least $174,000 a year. These salaries are paid by taxes.

A governor meets with state leaders to review the state budget.

Each year, the state governor looks at the money the state has. The governor and other leaders then plan how to use the money. This is called a *budget*. The biggest part of most state budgets pays for education and public welfare. This can help a local government build a school. It can help pay for programs for people in need. And it can pay the salaries of elected officials.

If there is not enough money to pay for everything, states can raise taxes or cut spending. And they will often get help from the federal **government**.

Think and Talk

Is it fair to have taxes? Explain your thinking.

Everyone who lives in a state can say how they think the state's money should be spent. But not everyone gets to directly make the decision. Even so, it's good to make needs known. For instance, at the local level, this can be as easy as talking to the principal of a school. At the state level, it might mean calling a senator's office. None of these leaders will know what the public thinks and wants if the people do not say so.

311

In many U.S. cities, a quick call to 311 is all that's needed to report a problem. This is a nonemergency number. Callers to 311 may be able to find out information about services. They can make complaints. And they can report problems such as a fallen road sign or graffiti.

If there is a crack in a street, anyone can call their local city office. If a state park is run down, people can let their park leaders know. Many places have websites to report problems or concerns. Local and state leaders often have offices to visit as well. People can call or write emails to their leaders, too.

Many local and state governments have money set aside for public concerns. If people think more money should be spent, they can ask. If they don't like how money is spent, they can make their voices heard about that as well. They can write letters, make calls, and protest. And voters can always select new leaders if they don't like how their leaders spend the public's money.

The government is responsible for repairing broken roads.

Federal Government

In the United States, the federal government works for all the people of all the states and **territories**. It pays for many things that are common to all Americans. For example, it manages food and drug safety. It invests in education. It invests in bridges, roads, and highways. The government may pay for transportation services. These might be planes, boats, or subways. It pays for people to inspect and repair these things as well.

A major part of the federal budget goes to **defense** and the **armed services**. The government also pays for itself. Many people work for the government. Their salaries are paid through taxes. The systems and places they run have to be paid for as well.

the USS *Gerald R. Ford*

The government offers aid, too. It helps people in trouble. It provides **Medicare** for people over 65 and with special needs. It provides **Medicaid** for people with low incomes, disabilities, and more. When disasters strike, it may send money and helpers. It also helps countries around the world that are in need. And when states need money, they may turn to the federal government. The federal government is only strong if states are strong. And states are stronger when the federal government is, too.

A Drop in the Bucket

Many items in the U.S. federal budget cost huge amounts of money. The whole budget is massive. For example, nearly $13 billion dollars was spent to build a single new aircraft carrier (the USS *Gerald R. Ford*). It costs millions every month to keep the carrier running. And this is just one tiny part of the whole budget!

People across the country may need help as well. The country offers many supports for people in need. One big need is paying for college. College can be costly. The United States has long supported education. So, the country budgets money for student grants and loans. A grant is money given to a student that they do not have to pay back. Students might earn grants because of good grades and special needs. A loan is borrowed money that a student pays back. Many students can afford to go to college with the help of grants and loans.

The government also pays Social Security **benefits** to people who **qualify**. Most U.S. workers pay into Social Security. Part of their paycheck goes to the fund. The money they pay is then paid out to people who receive benefits. Most often, these are people age 62 or older who have **retired**. The spouse or young children of someone who dies may also receive their benefits. Someone who has been injured or is too ill to work might also receive payments. The fund is meant to ensure that people who are no longer working have what they need to live.

Budget to Spending

A governor proposes a budget each year for the state. Then, the **legislature** approves it. The people in local towns can sometimes vote on how it is spent. They can write letters, call, or email. Sometimes, they really don't like how the money is being spent. In the next election, they can vote for different officials.

It works the same way in the federal government. The president of the United States looks at the money collected in taxes. They look at all the places that need the money. The president and their team make a budget. Congress approves it or asks for changes to be made. People in the states tell Congress how they want the money to be spent. In the end, Congress decides.

People have a say in how government spends money.

People in the United States share their thoughts on government spending.

In the United States, many people have a voice in how the money is spent. They can share their ideas and opinions. Businesses do this. Newspapers and news shows do this. Religious leaders and celebrities do this. Scientists and artists do this. People in every state and community do this. The president and other leaders hear what all these people have to say. Then, they try to make the best decision.

Who's the Boss?

Anyone in the United States can speak openly about what they think should be in the budget and how money should be spent. But the leaders that people elect actually make the decisions. Of course, the leaders are elected by the people. So, are the people or the leaders in charge?

The Deficit and the National Debt

In some years, the budget is balanced. For example, if you had $20 and you spent $20, your budget is balanced.

In most years, the government spends more than it makes. The difference is called the **deficit**. When the government has to borrow money, or if it spends more than it takes in, the total it owes is called the **national debt**.

If the government wants to spend $200 and only has $100, what can be done? How can it spend more money than it collects?

$28 Trillion

Over time, the U.S. national debt has climbed to a staggering amount of money. The interest payment on this debt each year is hundreds of billions of dollars. A big part of the U.S. budget goes to paying interest on debt.

THE NATIONAL DEBT
$27,169,129,876,097

Say your aunt wants to buy a car, so she takes out a loan. She has to pay back the loan plus a little bit extra. This extra money is called **interest**. A car that cost $10,000 might actually cost her $11,500.

When the government needs more money than it collects, it does not take out a loan. It issues debt. It pays this debt back. It also pays back a little extra.

Who buys this debt? People buy this debt. Companies can buy this debt. Other countries can buy this debt, too.

💡 **Think** _and_ **Talk**

What effects might there be from companies and other governments buying a country's debt?

Then and Now

The federal government worked to raise money even before the United States was a nation. It needed money to fight the **Revolutionary War**. Many people helped to make this happen. Alexander Hamilton was at the top of that list. He is one of the nation's Founders. He helped form the national bank. He also led the plan for the new nation's economic system. His picture is on the ten-dollar bill.

Alexander Hamilton

From the beginning, war and defense have been among the biggest national expenses. Together with healthcare, Social Security, and interest on debt, they make up about two-thirds of the federal budget.

the New York City skyline

The government has spent a lot of money through the years. It has spent money to build cities and roads. It has spent money on war. It has spent money on health and education. It pays for schools. It pays to keep the water and air clean. It pays for people to serve at all levels of government. And it pays for the buildings where they work.

It takes a lot to run a government! It always has, and it always will.

New York City

Hamilton worked to make New York the financial center of the United States, and it still is. Much of the nation's financial deals are made there. In fact, New York City is an important international financial center, too.

It's Everyone's Business

There are more than 300 million people who live in the United States! Everybody pitches in by paying taxes in one way or another. People also make their voices heard. This helps the government spend money in the best ways. Some people think the government should spend more money. Some think the government should spend less. Every voice matters when it comes to making these decisions.

There are many things that all or most people use. They use electricity and drive on roads. They or their children go to school. Everyone breathes air and drinks water, so it is important that they are clean and healthy. Can any one person or group take care of these things? No. It takes a whole group—the government—to do it.

The work we do together can make free time and plenty of opportunities for play!

Just like Anthony, who got money from his grandmother in "The Dunk Tank," each level of government receives money. And just like him, each level has to decide how to best spend it. Each has to find ways to raise more money, too.

The levels of government also work together. The federal government helps the states. The states help the cities or counties. The cities and counties help the neighborhoods. The neighborhoods help the people. The people tell the government what they need. The more they communicate with the government, the better the government can decide how to spend the money. In the end, it's everyone's business!

Glossary

armed services—military, naval, or air forces

benefits—money that is paid by a company or a government when someone stops working, becomes sick, or dies

defense—the part of the federal government that protects the nation from threats

deficit—the amount of money spent over what is collected

democracy—a form of government in which people vote for their leaders

federal—related to the one central government

government—a group of people and systems with ruling power

income tax—money collected from people's jobs

interest—extra money charged to pay for borrowing money

legislature—the branch of government that makes laws

Medicaid—a public insurance program managed by states that provides health coverage for certain people

Medicare—a public insurance program managed by the federal government that provides health coverage for some people

national debt—money that the government has borrowed or spends beyond what it takes in

property tax—money collected on buildings and land

qualify—to meet a required standard

retired—ended a working career

Revolutionary War—the war between Great Britain and its American colonies, 1775–83

sales tax—money added onto the cost of an item by the government for its use

territories—areas of land that belong to or are controlled by a government

Index

Civics in Action

Knowing how to budget is essential for government leaders. It is a great skill for you, too! Work together to create a budget for a classroom event. Here's how.

1. Choose an event for the class to host. Maybe it is an open house or a presentation for families and friends to see.

2. List items that must be purchased for the event. These might include decorations or snacks.

3. Make a spreadsheet. In the first column, list each item to be purchased. In the second column, list the item's estimated cost. In the third column, list the source of income. (This is how you will pay for it.) Maybe it will be donated. Maybe the class will have a fundraiser. Maybe the school has money in its budget for the purchase.

4. Can you balance the budget? Decide together if any item in the budget needs to change based on your income options.